# TRAVELOGUES

## ALSO BY KATHLEEN JENNINGS

Flyaway

## PRAISE FOR *TRAVELOGUES*

'*Travelogues: Vignettes From Trains in Motion* is a poet's plunge into an oil-slickered, shadow-hung, ivy-clung alternate reality. Jennings' world is deeply familiar and ultimately alien: a world minutely observed, in fast forward, warped by fairy lenses. Her reflections are relentless, ecstatic, declamatory, are illuminated motion. This whole metaphorical journey-by-rails is a fantasia, a phantasm, at times wistful, at others muscular and machine-like, with the occasional wry aside about the terribleness of the coffee. "Hello, book!" I want to shout. "I know you! And yet, I have never met your like." Let's never get to Salisbury. Let this train ride never end.'
—C. S. E. COONEY, WORLD FANTASY AWARD-WINNING AUTHOR OF *BONE SWANS: STORIES*

"*Travelogues* tracks between fairytale forest and human industry, refiguring the railway through the tender wildness of the everyday. Delightfully unexpected in their metaphors, as wrought in sound as in image, these poems embody our attention and our daydreams—casting new light, new shadows. Jennings makes magic of the detail and colour of the quotidian world, where a cluster of rust-wrecked cars are kindred with autumn leaves, where a bare tree twins curves of concrete, where a train is a knife slicing through butter-and-honey light. Nearly there, nearly there. A world at work, remade through window and motion. And further."
—SHASTRA DEO, *THE AGONIST*

# TRAVELOGUES

Vignettes from Trains In Motion

## KATHLEEN JENNINGS

Copyright © 2020 by Kathleen Jennings

All rights reserved. No part of this book may be reproduced in any form or by any electronic or mechanical means, including information storage and retrieval systems, without written permission from the author, except for the use of brief quotations in a book review. Kathleen Jennings asserts her right to be known as the author of this work

ISBN: 978-1-922479-00-6

Cover design by Peter Ball © Brain Jar Press

Cover Image: Vertyr, Shutterstock

Brain Jar Press
PO Box 6687
Upper Mt Gravatt, QLD, 4122
Australia
www.BrainJarPress.com

## Contents

| | |
|---|---|
| NYC to Northampton | 1 |
| Baltimore to NYC | 4 |
| NYC to Northampton | 9 |
| Exeter to Portsmouth | 13 |
| Exeter St. David's to Bristol Temple Meads | 15 |
| NYC to Northampton | 17 |
| Bristol to London | 21 |
| Paddington to Exeter St. David's | 25 |
| Northampton to NYC | 28 |
| | |
| Acknowledgments | 33 |
| About Kathleen Jennings | 35 |
| Thank You For Buying This Brain Jar Press Chapbook | 37 |

## NYC to Northampton

4 JULY 2016

How can people work on trains? Read on trains?
  There is so much happening outside: Trees and
  iron pylons, golf-cart graveyards, vines. Rapunzel-
  towers of overgrown silos, muralled with graffiti.
Forgotten windows, weeds and wildflowers, signs
  unclad.
Artichoke-leafed storeroom roofs; construction
  equipment out of old picture books. Lines and
  wires and insulators, brickyards and urban
  quarries.
Men under golf umbrellas in carparks. Abandoned
  cinemas, flags, the occult paraphernalia of sidings
  (arrays of buckets, lights, signs). Leaf & light &
  trunk & wire, chain-link fence & overpass, signal
  box & gate & stair.
Orange tape & rusted drum. Sleeper, chimney, lamp &
  stone. Sun-bright domes and needling spires,
  bridges arched like a skipped pebble.
A swooping net of cross-mown lawn, lilies yellow-
  starred on a cool olive sky, a trickle of creeks,

water clear as gasoline. The swift-tumbled bank
down to furtive trees.

A bridge like a shout of iron. Bee hives spindle-legged
—INDUSTRY—a piano-accordion.

Waisted pylons, leaves dense as a mattress. A spilling
warehouse where all the trash is stored.

School buses, corralled, yellow as waterlilies. And
willows, willows streaming in our wake. Willows
straining and effortless as sleep. Telephone poles
like a word game or a condemnation, flower-foam
frothed on embankments.

Shingles hammocked between rafters, a yard secretive
with conspiracies of pipes and funnels. Summer
piled thick as a symphony, leaf-pleated, pod-
smocked, buttoned with blossom and set about
with red-brick and tar.

Generous mysteries of warehouse doors, a cool
wilderness of concrete colonnades (and beyond,
towers cream and blue as Wedgewood, as pewter).

Immense scrollwork brackets, a freight-train painted
like wooden teething beads (red, cream, folk blue),
flowered with graffiti.

And clocks! Clocks on towers, gilt-shadowed; new-
grown sundials. A pendulum of wires, the chime of
horns, the ratchet-tick of miles.

And hello river, stone-tucked and snag-gathered! I
know you!

(Over that river the land becomes unsettling: oiled silk
water flocked and baized with algae, trees hot-
handed against the windows.

An inexplicable, almost intelligible script of bleached
trunks; even the bulldozers cluster, somnolent,
closer by the tracks, too yellow.)

It is the being-on of trains that I like. The way the

world(s) and people move around them. They pleat the world and weight time.

(And on: trucks engulfed by the slow embrace of vines, a field of chalk-pale satellite dishes listening, or watching—I think it is not accidental that they are bowed like the bowl of a camera obscura.)

I did not realise how ominous Massachusetts could look with all its leaves on. Beautiful still, but engulfing, like a green gullet.

There! A brand new platform, small as a cubbyhouse and smelling of fresh-cut timber. An electric violin tunes up at the cafe.

## Baltimore to NYC

5 NOVEMBER 2018

A yellow fog of rain and ochre leaves over a matte
    pewter bay. Not swooping—gliding straight and
    velvet as if between two walls of painted scenes.
The woods are chiffon, thin and hazy.
A tall white house alone in sere and tawny stubble.
The powerlines and industrial estates, the fallow fields
    of white trucks, the autumnal bulldozers and black
    plastic fencing. The toy houses set down anyhow,
    the large-boned fuel stations. All lost in the woods.
And the woods crowd up to the umber water.
And the towns are harbours in the trees.
A deep pile of wrecked cars fallen, rusty as leaves, at
    the base of a tangled hill.
The water breaks off into the ellipses of short-
    stumped jetties. When you are on the water, there
    is nothing but water. When you are in the forest,
    the world is made of trees. But the houses are built
    to keep both out, and the houses cannot forget.
The train sings like a finger on the rim of a glass.

# Baltimore to NYC

I think autumn is an invention, an infection.

Culverts and buttresses, cuttings and weighbridges, iron and concrete both softened and fall-stained. A pine-green shed, a turned-bone tanker. Both bleed and lichen and bloom.

At home it is spring, the variegated-rose bark is peeling like ribbon candy and the trees are shedding violet and scarlet like painted shade. Fall is made-up, like yellow schoolbuses, sororities and American high schools.

And Wilmington, Delaware. Someone has dreamed it up and neglected to fill in the details. The sky is blank as water and I don't know what will happen if you get off the train.

The doors ring like a distant alarm and a man gets on, out of the dream, with a hard hat and hung about with keys and carabiners. Why does he need so many? Where are the locks they open? What was out there?

On the other side of that high vine-knotted wall, a car company. Below that low bridge, a little river, warm-olive and silver.

Dredges, grave and solitary, and are they above the train? Are we a little heavier on the water? There is a ticket above me shaped like a bookmark. The conductor puts her hand on my shoulder. "If you decide to move, just move that with you."

A lady in a neat suit and gold necklace staggers down the aisle and here is a house, half soot and hanging shingles and half scarlet and icing-white, and the train cuts *between* the world and a railway is a wild, implausible idea.

These high, hunched houses, ornamented on two

sides, are shaped to press together, but each stands alone on its lawn, at offset angles, with its turrets and blank bay windows, and the trees pry between them.

Philadelphia, and a convocation of hi-vis vests might have been shaken from a branch onto the tracks.

Philadelphia, with a railway bridge putting out leaves and a willow brooding over a rubble pile.

An enclosed station belongs to the world of the carriage. It's an airlock, easier to believe.

"Yes, mountain bikes," "Yes, spin classes," "Yes, record stores," say the signs. You must build the city from that, and here is a perspective grid of lines and cables upon which to construct it.

It is unfinished. The tops of buildings are soft sketches in the clouds.

Narrow, pastel houses like used paperbacks. A factory hollowed out and refilled with rubble. The skeleton of a roof, the bound of great red-and-white arched windows. The codes of hundred-paned industrial windows, like so many palms: glass, black glass, empty, boarded-up.

Tall, pendulous-bellied tanks on mosquito legs, picking their way over factory roofs.

The raw ends of row-houses, depot yards, the cross-sections of the world.

An ill-knit, finger-knit shawl of vines, displayed between two power poles (knotted, drop-stitched).

Back into the trees. Push your face into the trees and hold yourself under until you can breathe again, and there is no city, only stray pale rectangles reforming and distorting on the surfaces of the world.

On two arches of a mint-green box-girder bridge,

dashing against the foliage: "TRENTON MAKES, THE WORLD TAKES."

The brashness of industry is a type of creative defiance. "Here, take. Come buy."

Do these houses feel permanent? Did the painter of the ANTIQUES sign know how unlikely it looks to claim, here, for these things, antiquity? The trees persist through impermanence. Turning. A stretch of pale bare trunks, and a pylon frozen among them.

Peach, cherry, lemon. Such full colours for something so thin as leaves.

A basket of gold, rustling, full as a heart.

Grape, loquat, mandarine. Pomegranate, melon. Plum, lime. Bark and paper.

On an embankment, a tyre holds down a white sheet of tin.

"174 to Boston."

Three bells.

MetroPark pretends a stately arrangement with the trees. A grand park. But the trees are taller here, and the wet, lion-coloured grass by the carpark is unkempt. The golf course has been manicured but the trees are otherwise engaged. Make, and change, and toss it down.

Plates of riveted tin patch the dome of a silo, rounded as if to fit a hand. No prefabricated pretence (without any seam or ironwork): here is a thing that was made.

The leaf-mould of old industry: mossy concrete, verdigris, wine-dark walls.

Newark, and a breeze only out the right-hand windows. One shrub waving wildly as its

neighbours stand still. A copper dome. A spire.
Safety rails harmonise with a pale yellow tree.

A gold dome, black-topped like a set pearl. Racks of
cars, neatly stored like the pieces of a game. And
here you begin to believe the towers are building
themselves into being; summoned as in a mirror,
they will resolve as you approach them, gain details
fractally.

The burnt-bark laminations of a railway bridge. The
concentric rings of a city.

In approximately ten minutes, ladies and gentlemen,
you, too, must become real again.

A toybox yard: trailers, boats, pick-ups, tumbled and
twisted. On a small black car in great letters:
LOST.

Here is a field of reeds, soft as sleep on the eyes. There
is the city half-suspended from cloud.

Say its name twice in the window and summon it.

White waterbirds, still.

The train calls like an indrawn breath.

A brick beehive with a temple door. A tunnel. Lights
flash by, counting down. And you will wake up,
any moment now.

[Photo: You have arrived]

New York!

Two men diligently sweep water uphill, and the
roofline is a case of faceted, opaque jewels.

## NYC to Northampton

### 16 NOVEMBER 2018

The train pulls out on an indrawn breath, in darkness,
  like the suspense of strings being tuned behind a
  curtain.
The world is being made. Plastic sacks of earth, of
  timber, of iron shards, of wires.
Five men frown at a flaming spar. The props of lives
  stored on flat roofs: buckets, ladders, a yellowing
  tree in a blue-glazed pot.
They are letting out the seams of the city.
Self-edged, selvedge, unhemmed, whip-stitched with
  cables and weighted with concrete, rolled with
  fraying vines, blanket-stitched with a scrabble of
  pickets, beaded with paper cups, knee-deep in
  river mud.
A fall forest waits like a fable.
Last week's gilding has tarnished. The trees are rusted
  and verdigrised.
The graffiti on the cuttings, arrows and obscure
  commands, are tailor's marks.
Sheds chained in back yards follow the train with unlit

windows. The nervous system of ivy displayed on a wall. The naked belly of a boat. Dissecting pins and wires hold the bloodless branches peeled away from the tracks.

These rusting sutures make an enormous creature, beautiful, unnatural. It rushes headlong into wastelands, blunders with unwieldy, clever brutality into the cities' hearts.

New York. New Rochelle. New Haven.

A bulldozer broods on a nest of gravel. Here is where they make. Here is where they store: water; sacks of leaves; pallets; iron staircases; the pewter sky in the broken mirrors of a swamp.

A small town. The fine, tidy houses face the line, the trimmed verge of the corridor. The train rolls on a mattress of leaves, then clatters back behind the arras, dragging the straggled carried-stitches at the back of the trees. Pressing against mismatched, milky factory windows, kicking through the trash.

At Bridgeport, the little boats have slid down their ramps and lie tangled together. There are so many broken factory windows and, within, the buildings are fretted and porous as a theatre. As if you could click a lever and the world would revolve inside them.

Here are trees broken into their component parts and sorted: bolls, branches, twigs, leaves.

Self Storage. Auto Body. Choose a name, guano-white, from the underpass and wade out into the dark water.

Gravestones thin as train tickets, or bookmarks, or garden markers.

At New Haven the train stops. The power is off. In the

grey afternoon twilight the passengers eat to keep warm.

From the train, you can see where all the car bodies are buried. We are leaving the leaves behind.

The train is a harmonica. Sucking cold air through the teeth of the trees, the one broad low note of someone testing a mouth-organ.

A blue truck, broken, in a hollow of brown. Rusted funnels and conveyors, spilling flakes.

A mirrored dragon, pink stomached, climbs a rail in Meriden and grimaces through its forest of teeth.

A plastic dollhouse falls open like a book beside the tracks.

Two car seats, a love-seat, settled on the bank. Waterlilies flat as palms against wet grass. Black trees against a red ground.

In Hartford a flare of paint hot as an after-image, and then red brick, red grass, red ox-blood boughs.

In a sheet of inky water, foam circles each tree as if they are continents on a map.

Not foam - ice! The puddles at a rest stop are cracked like car windows. (I've had five summers in a row, and really haven't packed for this.)

A yellow schoolbus like a jeep's fever dream. Snapped sugar lace on a boarded-up station building. A river dimpled like glass.

Trees cracked like marrow-bones. Membranous ice, and a duck standing ankle-deep, affronted. Thin sheets and shoals of layered ice and algae, and the bronze trees hanging over them, and the whiplash of a wrist-thick vine grown over the rail of an abandoned bridge.

Berries, amber and hematite, topaz and jasper and coral.

- Ochre and umber and ash. The only blue is the flat brow of an engine, a safety helmet, the indigo skull of a hill.
- In Springfield we slice through the geological ages of a train station. Bones of forgotten platforms. Dendrites of rebar.
- We draw back, like the tide, like a cord, like retreating depth of field (Under the bridge lives an abandoned signal tower.) Past the vast fretwork of a footbridge leading from lumberyard to empty lot. Under the spiked-mace finials and haloed lamps.
- And forward, past a frozen foam of berries, a surf of gravel and yellow grass. A passenger in the back of the carriage tells a story about the train he caught as a young man in Spain that went four hours in the wrong direction.
- The ink splutters and blots in the trees. We have always been leaving Springfield.
- Galaxies of ice spiral along the river, slow as the train's long note.
- Holyoke. A crest of pigeons huddled along the curve of a great rusting duct above an empty factory.
- The clouds are slung between church spires, like a damp fleece.
- A sudden, chafing urgency in the rhythm of the wheels. The water between reed-beds is ruched and shirred.
- An obsidian pond. A thin waterfall. A wintering wood. Nearly there. Nearly there. Nearly there.

## Exeter to Portsmouth

### 12 JULY 2018

It's hard to be unhappy on a train, though.
Trainspotting pheasants. Noonday ewes strewn unconscious beneath an oak.
Dark tunnels where time stands still, and bright tunnels of tossing leaves.
The sense of sliding on the shoulder of the world. The moiré of bracken, defiant banks of foxgloves, stone-coloured sheep in neolithic arrangements.
Rampant pale columbine, grasping briar. Red brick, blue-ochred slate. High-bounding old bridges, swooping new ones. Dark glossy rivers. Thin-spun, light-worn hills. Power pylons marching— more aloof, but no more unlikely, than the railway.
The recurring sense of riding through a Stephen Biesty book, or travelling into a popup volume with sliding tabs and hidden flaps. Not a two-dimensional world, but a chance to look at its inner workings.
Horizons receding and approaching so quickly you can feel the air compress as the pages turn.

(Like the introductory ride in Jurassic Park, and at any station you too could elbow your way out into the world.)

Hills as close and flocked as the clouds.

Really bad coffee.

A field of baled hay always looks like a grazing herd of cylindrical ruminants.

A tent in a field. An ornamental iron bench. A ragged net of crows lifting off golden straw.

Rabbit hutches, clotheslines, gardening sheds, picnic tables. Pallets and tractor hulks and signs for auto repairs. Hedgerows and woods and cows, which unlike sheep are always resolutely actors rather than scenery.

Let's never get to Salisbury.

Swans and flotsam, mud and yachts. Sleek curves and the swamp of shipping.

White swans waddling in single file along a channel in a weed-greened mudflat, while old sailboats recline on one elbow around them.

And then: The sea! The sea!

A blue wooden door under a blue iron bridge. Cranes and drowned shopping trolleys. Depots and pines. Laundry bannering triumphant.

Frayed English flags. A deflating flamingo. Headstones decorous through the trees. An umbrella on the tracks. Buddleias, abundant.

Portsmouth Harbour, and no further.

## Exeter St. David's to Bristol Temple Meads

8 AUGUST 2019

A spire receding into rain. Green eves.
A field hip-deep in flowers. Concrete troughs.
An idling of cows.
A caravan, a chicken hut, an oak (the answer: that they
    have in common awnings)
Thatch, slate, tile, and a spy-hole chimney
A tapestry of trees: woven through, stitched over,
    applied and tufted, darned-in, gold-nubbed, silver-
    shot, picked out in russet.
A yellow digger, a copper beech, and the eternal
    buddleia.
Charcoal-faced sheep burdened by the world's weight.
[Way out over footbridge]
The tufted pennants of a water-meadow; the
    overspray of the platform's edge misted like a bar
    of moonlight on the ballast.
Earth cut pink as chocolate cake. A dead sheep
    snagged like a bur in the grass.
The frank mysteries of allotments.
[If you must leave, go by train]

Sorghum red as bridges. Rook and raven; willowherb.
An oak pollarded like a crucifix.
A shard of a river. A glitter of willow.
Wires like a loom.
Broad, flat country now, and the streams open to the air. Shaded by a crow on a fence post.
Before, the hills rose up to the low sky. Now the clouds bend down.
Ponds and conservatories and pots of geraniums.
Broad flat factories and broad flat developments and wide, low solar farms.
Wide still rivers and straight rails like haematite, and perspective lines out of a textbook.
A hill at last, with houses off a hanging, and its top cut into banks and plateaus.
Rows of caravans, rows of rental cars, rows of poplars, the blank ends of houses.
Straight hedges, curved fences, crumbling sheds.
Rumpled country: a cutting, a tunnel, a bank. The swell of a wheat field, a splash of flower-foamed cottages.
Backyards and palings and footbridges. Blocks of colour, joined at the chimneys. Towers and palings and Bristol.

## NYC to Northampton

### 13 NOVEMBER 2019

Cue "Hall of the Mountain King": Dim and tangled caverns, hoarded pipes and wires.

A blast of sun, a scree of cables. A cement truck, yellow-and-white, big-abdomened as an ant.

The rusting secret cities of rooftops: fogged coffer skylights, vents battered but aloof. Dense, tame clouds of steam and a fraying sketch of flags. The clean, steep angle of an aeroplane.

From here, it is a low, bridge-stapled city, no higher than a freight of shipping containers. The river olive, indigo, gull-spangled. The trees hung with yellow coins.

The trees, the trash, the witch's hats, the shopping trolleys, the strata, the shadows, rushing headlong downhill.

Ironwork over the tracks, vine-wrapped, like a tale of castles.

Teal water slowly dismantling a barge, a seeping current of red leaves, lion-coloured reeds.

A storm of leaves, a bright tunnel, the train flying

upstream and ochre shards dash and strike the glass.

A slim, rust-scumbled silo rapunzeled by vines.

The strutted powerline supports are painted white now, and if they still look like fairy-tale palaces it is a 1950s version of them, tidy, the remaining leaves on their vines painted in gouache by a strong, sure hand.

A sudden blooming of rose windows. A yard piled with chairs like a bonfire of spinning wheels.

Late autumn, through glass, promises warmth: oven-red, honey-gold, baked-bread, water like treacle and the sun striking every twig like a match.

Substations strung like a loom, a barge trailing sparks.

Bulldozers carefully patting dirt into nests; ducks sleeping, suspended, in the shallows.

Doric-columned overpass. Garden sheds like temples in the trees.

A large grey dog, deliberate about some errand; small pools lacquered with leaves. Out of the woods runs a long white fence, but only the final few yards are bright with graffiti and greened with moss (and why did neither moss nor vandal go further into the trees?).

The low midday sun guards creek and pond and inlet with a flaming sword.

A hawk, unsteady on its level; a red willow-pattern creek; gunmetal, diesel-blue, oiled-silk water.

An organ-pipe cry. A beetle-wing blanket of carparks. Copper leaves, turned to look behind us.
Somewhere in the carriage, a single phone is ringing, ringing.

Grey, grave houses like headstones. The whalesong of

trains, the hollow-mouthed horn, more groan than scream.

Red stone cenotaphs. A moth-hail, again, of leaves.

Dead televisions gleaming like jet in the tumble of fall.
Chrysanthemums glowing on a balcony. Snarls and blots of nests in spidered trees.

Green slate and gold-leaf domes; stacked lumber & steel. Birches white as broken plasterboard; a foam of algae, flotillas of lily-pads with oil-calm water between them. Sleeping swans chilling one leg at a time.

How dark the water. How bright the sky.

Shredded paper, and birds rising like letters from it.

The rust is a brighter orange now, and the leaves are fewer. Sun glosses all but the classic cars and strikes a gilded dome like a bell.

Industrial decay, dignified by age: bole-red brick, arches swollen with wood, windows mosaic-ed with colour and darkness, an ebullience of graffiti blooming the same song the train sings: I am here, I am here, I am here.

Water tucked and smocked by stones. A net of orange beads, purple-stemmed briars, saplings in the bare woods putting on one last green burst of growth while the light is theirs.

Crossed-contrails combed back into wings, and a crow climbing against them.

Low light, slow slight, and something like ice in the river?

Wood-lace porches, harvest wreaths, a yard with a dozen bird houses.

Old graves and rubbish spill into a ditch. Men in hi-vis are picking the hooves of cranes.

On one side, strong flat blocks of colour. On the other,
   a river etched in white fire and oxidised silver.
An efflorescence of arabesques on finials, capitals,
   lamp posts.
A bare tree beneath an overpass echoes the curves of
   concrete. Above, a lamp — already on — burns
   against the warm blue sky.
(We have always been side-lined in Springfield.)

While we waited, the fiery river turned to pastel and
   vermeil.
Films and rinds of ice.
The river in shadow and the far shore gold. The
   turning hills streaked amber and twilight.

## Bristol to London

### 12 AUGUST 2019

The sweep of fields, carved angular and golden in the old light.
Then a tunnel and a green curtain, lilac turrets, an impossible country.
Piled gardens, a macrame of drainpipes. Long, cool, pale buildings and a frame of trees.
Another tunnel, and the enchanted country of Bath, with its rows of houses like rising castles, is wiped away: breath on a window. Here, instead, is a tangle of briars and brambles, the stately stride of pylons. Little spilled towns mounded with foaming clouds.
A heavy-bellied, fine-footed, low-jowled, spotted pig, grazing in a field.
(An old English pig, off a jug or a sign, stately and self-content.)
("All that a pig is, is perfect in the pig...", as Judith Wright did not say.)
The soft verticals of willows, the wandering arms of

oaks, futures sliding one after another, in a
ripening field.

Pleasant land, farming land, wheat heavy and
fingerprinted with wind.

Lemonade light, lavender shadow. An equine
conference. Blue smoke by a sawmill.

Easy-limbed hedges. Hawthorns clutching at nothing.
From a fold in the hills, a church's narrowing spire.

Boxcar-family clouds slide by, violet-bellied. Islanded
weeds brood on black water. Goats and horses face
off through a fence.

At a station, a man with a backpack and heavy boots,
wearing pale blue overalls, sits primly on a yellow
tool-box. In the carriage, a blonde woman with
heavy lashes drinks wine and eats chocolate.
Young, in a forest-green velour tracksuit.

The Americans in the next bay of seats have
established which among them are old enough to
know Roger Miller's "England Swings," and have
settled into companionable murmurings.

Sun on the crest of blackberries.

Now and then a tree leaps forward out of an etching,
pulling centuries of print history into the world
with it.

Bales scattered across a field like chequers. Silage
ribbed like a grill.

Meringue clouds. You could scoop out handfuls of
them. Sheep scattered with improbable regularity.
All heads down, as if they were identical models
carefully set out on a map.

The smooth running side-leap of a green overbridge.
Small woods, deeper on the inside, so dense and
dark on the smooth gilt land.

We have turned our cheek to the sun. The harvested

fields are tarnished. The trees hold up the fence and the fence holds up the trees, and a yellow hill rises up so near and smooth, right under our elbow, that it is like sliding down a dune.

The town lands, hard, at the edge of a weedy field. Half-timbering, the houses ruled out in black and white, and then a stone urn of a building. A sports field ringed with white pennants, strung high from light to light.

Factory skylights angled grimly up, neither reflecting nor harvesting the light.

READING.

Row after row of trains, like a rust-and-diesel way-station for timelines.

The light is warmer now. Not marmalade, but butter-and-honey. The sky in a river is shockingly cool, and the allotments are all-through sunflowers.

The swift banks blur; green velocity, railway time.

A shadow-space through the world, only a passing train to pull and buffet.

Narrowboats along wide water, under still dark trees. The intimate individuality of close-quartered yards. Wading pools, canals pushed between garden walls.

Urban reeds, welders, mantling leaves, rose-grown concrete beams and a pace like a low hum.

The world reduced to archways. The dry skin of a building, all else tossed like confetti.

A sandbox development. Chimneys, each jaunty with an aerial.

Domed views, and weary carriages.

A great laundry shed, gaudy with linen trucks. A pale,

sunken town, drowned through trees. Water low as
a gutter. Playground, spire, bell.

Rusted rails, hot with graffiti. And ivy; and ivy. An
oxidised memory of bracken, in this shadowless
half-world.

Stations we do not stop at. Houses that turn away.
Bridges that cross over. Blank-faced trains on
sidings.

Suddenly, we have already always been in London.

We are now approaching London Paddington, where
this train terminates.

## Paddington to Exeter St. David's

### 24 JULY 2019

Buddleia and verdigris. Rivets and linden.
Box bridges and chimneys, a heat-haze and pollen, red
    bricks and red buses. A semaphore of cranes.
Clouds like steam. Green silos, green hedges, a fire-
    work explosion of hi-vis vests.
Willows swooning melodramatically in the glare.
    Chimneys sturdy as stumps, poplars regimented
    like chimneys.
Wheat yellow as a page. Bright row-boats, leaf-
    drowned.
READING. It's certainly a station.
Leaves combed-back, silver-side out. The beginnings
    of a warehouse, bright as the picked-clean bones of
    a whale. Wheat all whiskery, stacked like coins. An
    exuberance of contrails.
Thatch and brick and a tiny church on a hill, all
    shaken out of a toile.
Cars parked neat and shiny as if pinned to a board.
Buddleia, foxgloves, columbine. Cool gullets of leaves

sloping down towards water. Copper beeches dark as a bruise.

Cattle wading in flowers. Allotments as simultaneously orderly and untidy as the string of canal boats.

Open fields, the world wiped clean, and the hills tilt and swoop up like a Ravilious.

Horses idle nose-to-tail, the better to keep off flies.

And then, sudden and wonderful on a hillside, keeping pace, a real chalk horse.

Cows, placid, black as oak-shadow, white as birch. Sheep like burrs in the grass. The massive, shouldering stillness of a summer countryside. A field of wrapped bales, like a backgammon board. Mossy thorn, a flash of blue (sky in a stream? a tarpaulin? the trim on a narrowboat?)

Half-blown thistles, ridged & ringed like festive fortresses, and ragwort bright as fresh paint. Gravel and briar. Rust and bramble.

And the train slides by like a knife through warm butter.

Barley sugar signal lights, butterscotch grass.

And real clouds, low and lilac. An amber glow of sunlight trapped in a tangle of trees. The backs of signs, round as pilgrims' palms.

How deep the shadows are under the trees on this bright day. Holes in the gilded air. Velvet as the end of the world.

Mostly full of cows.

A deer! A deer! A little russet thing, fine-boned, alone in long grass.

Vineyards, lenticular. The tops of vans glide along the hedges like the bubble in a spirit-level.

Geese! Dense as titanium white. Mobile phone towers,

abrupt, unreal, like waypoints in a game. Solar panels like a thing unnamed, as if the world is still under construction.

The hills lean and the trees lean and the train tilts sideways, and the sunlight pulls the heart out of the chest with yearning. As if the train won't meet the curves of the sky, the gather and tide of distances, and so you are the thing that must give.

Now cupped in a tunnel, now rumpled and unrolled almost to a sea-blue horizon.

A tent, an orchard, a tractor grumbling ahead of its load of hay. A ruin on a hill. A helicopter slow as a dragonfly. Churches in charcoal and goldenrod.

I want to memorise it all, but I can't. Try to catch hold and it rips past like rope.

Fields. Tawny as old velour. Glinting like ironed linen. Rippling like cat fur. Sheep-shorn and angular. Even-grooved as if thrown on a wheel.

In the pewter-mortared twilight of a tunnel, arched doorways press back into darkness like a promise, like the after-image of those bright ruinous breaks in hedgerows.

Cricket, bleached, and a single figure pink-shirted in the stands.

Clouds like breakers now and, lower, clouds like thistledown. Real patchwork hills. Sheep like silkworm cocoons. Greenhouses. Sunflowers. A crow caught in a current of air.

Stepping stones, pylons, and tracks braiding together. Then: Exeter St David's.

## Northampton to NYC

1 DECEMBER 2019

I.

The ponds are rimmed with frost, like salt, and filmed
  with ice, like a cat's eye.
A grisaille day, a sepia-wash day, a froth of white
  startling under a brick archway.
River like old tin. Snow clouds bleed and crystallise —
  Payne's grey, umber — and the varnish on the day
  is darkening.
The low curve of the bridge is mint-green, ice-cream
  green, and here's a gazebo cantilevered out over
  the water: two green garden chairs and a graphite
  shadow.
Leafless vines vein bricked-in windows, FLOUR
  dusted white on a wall, the glass in upper arches
  Wedgwood and marble blue.
Snow-cloud light is hail-and-bushfire light: a heavy,
  humid overlay; tobacco-stained sky; trees like bad
  lungs on a cigarette packet.

## Northampton to NYC

If warmth weren't still prickling back into my feet, I might not believe it's cold outside, instead of the end of the world.

Snow scrapes the trees off the sky, and red berries rattle past the window.

The snow is scratching away the world.

The train lows, and rust falls from iron trees; it flakes from a reddening bridge, a city of chipping russet.

A factory tower, cathedral-windowed, with a wide still moat and a wall of vines, tangled with the shopping bags and drink cans of all who have passed.

A sour cold, the shouldering nearness of a vacant train, looking through doubled, dark windows like smoked quartz. Ashfall, between carriages, of snow. The river like an antique mirror, a painted paper screen.

Tea-stained, coffee-water day, scraped-back pale on the tops of branches, the furrowed fields salted.

The berry-vines and brambles bend dark and shaggy under grey dust. Feathered reeds curled and powdered like wigs. The ground is red and the air is ivory and the trunks are murky green.

II.

We stop for a train to pass with a sound like time reversing. The snow rises. We proceed at a heart's beat.

Enamel day.

Snow unrolled and cut like felt. Snow poured-in like milk or plaster.

The river crests and crawls and tosses like a
   tarpaulin. The far shore is very far, and unfinished.
Surely the dried-blood iron bridge is warm, and the
   white road swift.
Tyres spilled downhill like bowls, old cars settling, a
   bookcase full of snow.
Lights in windows, the colour of cheap white wine. A
   chimney enshrined in glass, a chimney alone in the
   snow. Weak lemonade lamps, and bruised-lavender
   clouds.
Over two parking lots, a hundred crows lifting and
   circling, as fragmented and glossed as burnt paper.
The vaulted ceiling of a bridge, and a yellow bicycle
   gleaming like an ornament under station lights.
Tarnish and gleam. The guards tread snow through
   the carriage, and the windows are deckle-edged.
Through a stone arch, chandeliers. Folded cherry-
   pickers lurk like trebuchets under an
   overpass. Twilight bats against the windows. The
   schematics of the world fog and blur.
The train is a cold silver mouth-organ.
The train is a glass harmonica.
The train slides on the rim of a blue bowl, singing.
4:23pm phosphoresces like a movie midnight. Train
   yards like a velvet painting. Ceiling roses, hanging
   globes, the great iron wheel of a clock.
Across a platform, people read in amber.


III


Night, and all the shape of the land is in the shift and
   wallow of the carriage.

And the pattern of the rails beats at the base of the skull.
And in the carriage, a dog begins to howl.
Beads and strings of light, and night through specks of rain.
Coloured signs now. Black sequins, windows like a tortoiseshell comb.
Nets of holiday lights thrown over trees, the city fractal, recursive.
The train turns off its lights and glides, furtive.
It perches, silent, on a dark rooftop. Red lights below.
Then slips towards Penn Station.

## Acknowledgments

These recountings began as long threads of observations on Twitter, passing the time on trains (on which I can never settle to reading long books — there are too many things to see), and describing the landscape as it passed.

These threads became regular exercises. In order to make myself draw when I travelled, I had deliberately deskilled as a photographer, and these chains of snapshots played the same role as my pocket sketchbook: a process of keeping the mind and fingers warm; an attempt to capture the fraught but romantic intersection of the industrial and natural worlds; a reckoning with the unlikelihood of the railways as a concept; a study of scenes I want to remember; a sifting-through of lines and angles, metaphors and ways-to-see, until I found a pleasing ripple in the glass. And, unexpectedly, a hand extended across the miles to brush the hands of friends who recognised an allusion, a sentiment, or a place.

I'd like to thank everyone who, through encouragement, enablement, opportunities, responses, and/or spare bedrooms contributed in some way to these journeys, especially Kelly Link, Gavin Grant, Amal El-Mohtar, C. S. E.

Cooney, Ellen Kushner and Delia Sherman, Elizabeth-Jane Baldry, Terri Windling, several consecutive World Fantasy Conventions, the Diana Wynne Jones conference, and the Rencontres de l'Imaginaire de Brocéliande — and not forgetting South West Trains, Great Western Railroad, and Amtrak. Most particular thanks, of course, go to Peter M. Ball and Brain Jar Press, who wrestled a number of untidy documents of extracted tweets out of my hands, knocked off the roughest corners, and turned them into this book.

## About Kathleen Jennings

Credit: Ngaire Naran

Kathleen Jennings is a writer and illustrator based in Brisbane, Australia. Raised in western Queensland, she grew up either reading or staring out windows at trees on long drives, and long-distance travel has never lost its romance for her. She once wrote an honours thesis on railways in British children's novels, and now (in years other than 2020) spends many hours carrying art across other countries while half-reading poetry she picked up in towns at either end of train journeys.

Her debut Australian Gothic short novel *Flyaway* was published by Tor.com (USA) and Picador (Australia) in 2020 (and it does have illustrations). As an illustrator, she has been shortlisted four times for the World Fantasy Awards, once for the Hugos, and once for the Locus Awards, as well as winning a number of Ditmars. As a writer, she has won two Ditmars and been shortlisted for the Eugie Foster Memorial Award and for several Aurealis Awards. She completed an MPhil in Creative Writing (Australian Gothic literature) at the University of Queensland in 2019, and has since begun a PhD.

She can be found online at tanaudel.wordpress.com.

 twitter.com/tanaudel
 instagram.com/tanaudel
 patreon.com/tanaudel

## Thank You For Buying This Brain Jar Press Chapbook

To receive special offers, bonus content, and info on new releases and other great reads, visit us online at www.BrainJarPress.com

www.ingramcontent.com/pod-product-compliance
Lightning Source LLC
Chambersburg PA
CBHW021453080526
44588CB00009B/836